My First Poems

Volume One

by

Roy V. Benson

To george from Roy

Bloomington, IN   Milton Keynes, UK

authorHOUSE®

AuthorHouse™
1663 Liberty Drive, Suite 200
Bloomington, IN 47403
www.authorhouse.com
Phone: 1-800-839-8640

AuthorHouse™ UK Ltd.
500 Avebury Boulevard
Central Milton Keynes, MK9 2BE
www.authorhouse.co.uk
Phone: 08001974150

First published by AuthorHouse 3/13/2007

ISBN: 978-1-4259-7335-3 (sc)

Library of Congress Control Number: 2006910500

Printed in the United States of America
Bloomington, Indiana

This book is printed on acid-free paper.

I Met A Man, A Gentle Man

I met a man, a gentle man
Along the road one day
They called him Ron, that was his name
I met along the way

I'm 83, he gave to me
A dream that would come true
He told me in his gentle way
My life it isn't through

Our loving Lord He touched my life
I cannot here explain
I am so grateful for that man
I'll never be the same

A Bible Book Store opened up
It's all because of Ron
I saw the opening on that day
The breaking of the dawn

He made an old man's dream come true
That day that here we met
O yes he blest my life so much
I never shall forget

I met a man, a gentle man
He made my dreams come true
I guess my Lord is telling me
I have some more to do.

-Roy V. Benson, September 2006

Table of Contents

THESE POEMS

These poems to others, laugh as they may
"A foolish old man was he"
but a story they tell, my innermost thoughts
They're very important to me

If Only I be, the one which to read
to mull over their very thoughts
then they have served, each poem very well
they've given the peace that I've sought.

Each poem that I write, my thanks be to God
for my life, beginning to end
for all that I want, the end of this life
my days with my God to spend.

So these are my poems, they mean very little
But to God and I they mean much
for they're sung in praise, my spirit to raise
My life, I place in His trust.

If e'er you should read, these praises I've sung
In poem, to my Jesus above
I beg that you look beyond each mistake
These Poems that were written in love

VERY SINCERELY

ROY V. BENSON
(Circa 1960)

"BLESSED IS THE MAN WHO FEARS THE LORD ... HIS
HEART IS STEADFAST, TRUSTING IN THE LORD."
PSALM 112:1b, 7b

Roy V. Benson

MANSION BUILDING

I've seen some mansions here on earth
their building glorify
but did they build or even think
of mansions in the sky?

I wonder what their thought had been
to build such huge estates
I only hope they gave some thought
of Heaven, fore too late

To think the masses they could feed
The heartaches they could ease
if others they would give some thought
instead themselves to please

But it goes on and always will
It's just the same today
for man will only think of self
in his own selfish way

I think a joke when rich man gives
He gives for all to know
He wants his deed well glorified
He deeds, he wants to show

So what's your gain upon this earth
A mansion here below
or pass them up for better things
A mansion there to know

Lay up your wealth in Heaven above
The dividends live on
They even live upon this earth
Long after you are gone.

I HAD A FRIEND

I had a friend, or so I thought
Until the very day
He moved along then I found
It didn't come out that way

I thought him loyal at the time
He covered it so well
But it is odd that things come out
And time will finally tell.

I had no animosity
I bear him no ill will
And if he's need a helping hand
I guess I'd help him still.

I guess I cannot understand
That he'd do this to me
But it is odd how things come out
for every one to see.

But time will take and equalize
All wrongs to fellowman
We must forgive and understand
It's selfishness in man

THE INNER MAN

Is it right for me to live
to think of self alone
to want for things I have no need
to like my heart a stone?

Is it right to live a life
to feed this inner man
forget the needs of those about
as selfishly I plan?

When will this inner man be fed
so that he wants no more
when will desires have an end
when will he feel secure?

Oh friend, there is no end to self
He can't be satisfied
For if he owned the earth below
He'd reach into the sky.

So look about and lend a hand
to those about in need
this inner selfish man will die
when self you do not feed.

It is more blessed that you give
to help your fellowman
You'll gain much more. A life that's good
such joys you've never planned.

MINE, ALL MINE

The future's mine, completely mine
It's mine to lose or gain
to live a life that makes it mark
or mine to live in vain

I have the power deep within
to live as I dare please
But what have I when I look back
when this old life has ceased

I can forget all others bout
and feed this inner man
to crowd this life with this and that
do all for me, I can

But what the gain or is it loss
A loss I'm sure to be
for selfish thirsts cannot be quenched
no joy in self I'd see

So I can say only find my joy
to others I be kind
then I will live a life complete
with happiness to find.

CLAIM

Claim the promise of the Lord
Claim Him at His Word
Claim the promises that he gave
Each promise that you heard

A promise cannot be of good
Until that promise claimed
so therefore reach and hold onto
the promise in His Name

You see my friend, it's up to us
What more could He have done
He promised, then if we don't act
These claims cannot be won

So claim His promise, He will act
Reach out, it's yours to claim
He gives so freely in His love
So claim within His Name

So when you claim, believe it so
and then be patient still
it comes about in God's due time
This promise He will fill

MY INVESTMENTS

A pessimist I'm really not
This life on earth I love
But I have placed this trust of mine
With Christ, in Heaven above.

I feel secure invested there
No thieves, in Heaven to steal
My dividends will grow and grow
Invested wise I feel

It's just this world so shaky be
Investments here can lose
I'd rather place them with my Lord
Invest for him to use

The market's up and then it's down
There's silver and there's gold
Invest in this, but I don't know
I bought but should have sold.

There's experts in all fields today
Advise can come so cheap
They'll tell you how to make the most
Or monies you can keep

You ask each man no two alike
They all mean very well
Invest it here or over there
They all have things to sell

But then I think what is the best
Investment all around
Where will my gain be best fore me
Security be found

Roy V. Benson

Well, I met one, His name is Christ
He asked that I invest
In Heavenly things, where all is safe
And dividends the best.

And then I think how very short
In time, a vapor here
So if my treasures are laid up
In Heaven, I'd have no fear

I like to think they'll never fade
These dividends will live
And only grow for evermore
The more to him I give.

So every man should make a choice
The wisest he can make
For one will trust the Lord
Invest for Heaven's sake.

I KNOW NOT WHY

I know not why, the reasons for
these storms across life's path
I only trust Thy love for me
No greater love I have

I know the future's in Thy hands
come what, I need not faint
I know You'll keep me 'til that day
I gather with the saints.

Oh Lord, it gets so lonely here
My heart cries out to Thee
and yet I know You seest, Lord
Your heart goes to me

So Lord, I know not why or where
But yet I'll trust Thy ways
Until I gather at Thy throne
that bright and glorious day.

Roy V. Benson

THOSE WORDS

Those words you spoke the other nite
Those words you said to me
I hope you meant them not my dear
Those words said hastily

I know upset, you surely were
But words won't go away
those words you said, they found their mark
they seem with me to stay

You've never said you're sorry once
perhaps you meant each word
I'm sure if sorry you had been
By now, I would have heard

Those words can drive a wedge between
Such damage they can do
I'd rather not have words my dear
Especially with you

But as I said, I guess they're meant
Those words that came my way
and now I'll pray that they will pass
And we forget that day.

Oh words, oh words, what mighty power
The power to destroy
to rob us all, of things we want
to rob us of our joy

Those words, those words, those mighty words
The hurt that they can do
Those words we live, oh what a shame
those words cannot undo

So if we'd weigh each mighty word
to know it can destroy
but used in love how much it gives
to our Eternal joy.

Roy V. Benson

OH GUARDED TONGUE

I've never really gave it thought
What seeds, our words may be
We'll never know the hurt they've done
Until the harvest see

These words, so small but mighty too
These words we say in haste
What hurt, what wounds a word can make
Such goodness they can waste

Words are seeds, a harvest grows
What will the harvest be
It is all that we would want
The harvest we will see

Oh that we think and say good things
Then we would surely know
Our harvest would be all we want
From seeds we daily sow.

So guarded tongue and guarded words
I pray my portion be
For I would like a harvest great
A harvest great to see

WORDS WE SAY

It seems that others used to trust
We did not weigh each word
But now today is different still
They weigh each word that's heard

Distrust, I'd say, distrust of man
It's not a pretty sight
When every word a man might say
would cause some men to fight

Perhaps the world has changed enough
Our words yea or nay
Oh what a pity we've arrived
to weigh each word we say

So yea or nay, what more be said
Each word weighed carefully
Oh what a shame to live this way
what will the outcome be?

GOOD MORNING FRIEND

Good morning friend, another day
A brand new day unfolds
We cannot see just down the road
Just what this day may hold

But it is great to be alive
To hear the sparrows sing
And I would like to look for good
In almost everything

A brand new song this day will sing
I trust I catch its tune
I realize the time slips by
To pass so very soon

So may I say, "Good Morning, Friend
I pray a pleasant day
Be light in heart and carry on
in things you do and say"

LOOKING BACK, I MEANT RIGHT

In looking back, I thought I did
Do right, to others there
But I've been told it isn't so
I really didn't care

I've had an onslaught of such words
And if these words be true
Then I have failed this life I lived
In things I tried to do

I really meant to be so kind
To help, where help I could
I never really meant to harm
To harm, I never would

But words you see can make their mark
A cutting edge have they
I am sorry man my friend
If true these words they say

I never meant no harm to man
And yet these thoughts I live
of all these words that I have heard
My life, no good to give

I guess we cannot judge ourselves
others have that choice
It's better that we silent stand
and never raise our voice

So friend and foe and loved one too
Forgive, I ask of you
I thought I did, I really did
do best, my best for you

Roy V. Benson

You see I searched so very hard
If someone could love me
But all I did was fail them
This love, would never see

I only hope the Lord be kind
Forgive, I only pray
And maybe there, in Heaven's Courts
I then will find my way.

CUTTING WORDS

These cutting words that we pass on
We say to friend and foe
I wonder if we realize
The hurt they really show

Each cutting world will find its mark
a cutting sword be they
If only we would realize
These were in anger say

I fully know that I've been wrong
This guilt I too must share
for I have said some things to men
Some things not really fair

So if I could realize
The hurt that words can do
O pray that I may guard my tongue
And words of hurt be few

So cutting words, the harm they do
We'll never really know
But they remain, we may not see
They hurt may never show

17

MAD

A way of life it seems today
That everyone is mad
Oh what a shame to live this way
It seems so very sad.

Most everything their wants they have
They do not live without
But they complain that this is wrong
They rant and rave and shout

They're mad at this or mad at that
They're mad at everyone
They blame you for what may go wrong
For everything that's done.

So mad they are, a pity seems
To live this way my friend
But this they'll live, it is their way
They'll live it till the end

Reverse itself, I think it no
This madness only grows
For madness seems a way of life
This madness that they show.

IS IT FAIR

Some folks live just bathed in wealth
Others live the best of health
Some folks live with diamonds rare
I wonder if these things are fair

Some folks never give a thought
of things they've sold or things they've bought
They have no worries day to day
It must be nice to live that way

I wonder if they realize
How very little money buys
How some must struggle every day
Their daily bills in hope to pay

Is it fair the way they live
the more they get the less they give
they'll never know the feelings why
they'll live secured until they die

So some folks live a life of ease
themselves alone to only please
I guess they feel they have their share
and yet I wonder, is it fair?

Roy V. Benson

WHAT A PITY

A hundred million dollar plus
A wealthy man was he
You'd think the world would offer much
So happy he would be

This story's true, I'm telling you
in wealth he did abound
But all in vain this life he lived
No happiness he found.

Reverse came, he lost one third
A fifty million plus
His wealth meant everything to him
In it, he put his trust

To think a third he now had lost
His loss he thought too great
He found no reason why to live
This life of his to take

What a pity, what a shame
in millions, did abound
but all that wealth, and empty life
No happiness he found

It makes you wonder why this man
could not find reasons why
to spend his wealth, enjoy this life
and yet would rather die.

I'll tell you why, he placed his trust
In things, that turn to sand
for earthly things can never pass
the test of time to stand.

OUR TREASURES

Wherein do our treasures lie
What's dear to us on earth
What value do we place on things
What do we count their worth

What if these treasures disappeared
each one, no value there
Then could our heart be satisfied
Then could this life we bear

We have no guarantee my friend
these treasures have our name
what if they'd disappear my friend
would life be then the same

Why do we live as though they're ours
these treasures we count dear
I wonder if they'd mean the same
When death draws near

"What is their worth, my dying friend"
these treasures of the earth
are they all you thought they were
what is their real worth

I'd almost this his answer be
"those treasures be as sand
they'll never really past the test
The test of time to stand"

So choose your life and live it such
Your treasure, what's their worth
will they live on the ages long
or left behind on earth

21

CONSIDER WELL

Isn't it strange what some will do
For a bit of personal gain
It matters not to them one bit
the rules of the game

Of Yes, they'll promise anything
if it would gain them well
and they believe, I do declare
these stories that they tell

It truly is a shame that "things"
would cause a man to lie
for all those "things" will count for naught
The day he has to die

So we should all consider well
if gains are really gains
and if we're fair and played it well
The rules of the game

THE VERY BEST

Trips abroad and fancy furs
and hands bedecked with jewels
The very best of everything
The very best of schools

The very best in fineries
the best of foods to eat
well trained and groomed so properly
for every man you meet

The very best that life can give
the best of everything
the poor and meek will dance your song
your praises have to sing

A pittance here, you will cast forth
to quell their starving song
your riches great are yours alone
to no one else belongs

O foolish man, your day will come
your very best be gone
Then you alone will take your turn
to dance the piper's song

Roy V. Benson

LIVING HIGH

Is there a reason we should live
so high upon the hog
when others live below the line
of some American dog?

Is this right and is it just
The lot that some must live
but we could raise their lot in life
if we in love would give?

So think my friend, what do you count
Wherein your treasures lie
would they live on eternally
in case that you would die?

We all could give far more my friend
this guilt is ours to share
we live so high upon the hog
As though we do not care

I cannot point at you alone
I too, this guilt must share
I could do more for other men
for others, show I care

A LITTLE BIRD

He sings so early in the morn
This friendly little bird
He sings to God in Heaven above
The sweetest song I've heard

He raises loud his little voice
Another morn to see
He sings his praises for this day
How happy he must be

I think a lesson here to learn
each morn, we too should sing
for we have now the chance to see
Just what this day will bring

And I am of this thought my friend
Why don't we do the same
Why don't we sing our praises high
To not, is such a shame

Roy V. Benson

TO MY SON

I'll tell you this, my son, to learn
forgiveness in this life
this little word, so very big
will keep you out of strife

It isn't much as words may go
but yet it is the key
for only if you practice this
much good you'll live to see

It may not sound so hard to do
but yet it means so much
for Son, if you cannot forgive
Life's joy by you will rush

So Son, I say you must forgive
It's from the heart you know
you'll find such joy and peace abounds
that extra mile you go

I say this Son, I love you so
A joy you've been to me
I'm glad my God sent you along
in you such good I see.

A POET NOT

I cannot figure why these poems
A poet I am not
I only like to put them down
These lessons I've been taught

I really like to sing my praise
This way, to God above
I fully realize that these things
Are products of His love

Oh, I may tell in poem, my friend
some thought that's on my mind
I guess I really mean no harm
These thoughts I put in rhyme

So if they cause no harm to man
Perhaps they won't be read
They're only thoughts that I've put down
Some things I've done and said

And as I said, a poet not
So friend, be kind to me
and overlook just what you find
Mistakes, I know you'll see

So praises sung, that's what they are
our thoughts that cross my mind
expressions put in poem form
expressing thoughts of mine.

I'VE GATHERED IN POEM

I've gathered in poem, my thought of the day
I've gathered in poem, the words that we say
I've gathered in poem, the things on my mind
I've gathered in poem, the things that I find

I've gathered in poem, not everything gay
I've gathered in poem, the games people play
I've gathered in poem, the hurt that we give
I've gathered in poem, the way people live

I've gathered in poem, the beauty I see
I've gathered in poem, the beauty so free
I've gathered in poem, His praises to sing
I've gathered in poem, His praises to bring

I've gathered in poem, each hope that I hold
I've gathered in poem, my story be told
I've gathered in poem, the thoughts that I know
I've gathered in poem, these thoughts here to show

I've gathered in poem, you may not agree
I've gathered in poem, to things that I see
I've gathered in poem, enjoyment is mine
I've gathered in poem, the things that I find

So gathered in poem, for better or worse
Gathered in poem, in some kind of verse
Gathered in poem. This message I send
Gathered in poem, my message, my friend

MY FAITHFUL FRIEND

He thinks not of my faults alone
He thinks not "Has he failed"
He shows no evil in his eye
He only wags his tail

He's always ready to forgive
He never carries hate
He knows no malice in his heart
In anger never waits

Divorce, he knows not of the word
He shares my joys as well
And if I lonely feel at times
He seems to always tell

So faithful is this little friend
He'll stand through thick and thin
Such lesson learned from just a dog
But faithful to the end.

He's just a dog but what a friend
He cannot write or read
You see My Lord created him
He knew a friend I'd be

Roy V. Benson

HOW QUICKLY

These things of earth go quickly by
They last but for a day
They're here today, but disappear
they quickly fade away

Where is the joy, the peace man seeks
Where is the goodness found
we foolish men, we think we'll find
they joy in things around

But there is only joy in one
He gives His peace in love
When we in humble love submit
Our hearts to Him above

For here alone and only here
Doth joy and peace abound
In Christ, for only in His love
In Him, doth it abound

YESTERDAYS

I ne'er can live the yesterdays
The things that I did wrong
The one I hurt in foolish ways
The paths I walked along

I ne'er can live the yesterdays
The places or the things
Nor live on thought of days gone by
I cannot change a thing.

I can however, live today
to try to make it good
to let good deeds go forth in love
to treat it as I should

I can however, ask of those
The one I wronged those days
forgiveness, and in turn I must
put forth the same today

I cannot live tomorrow yet
I know not what it brings
for if I live, I pray to do
my best, in everything

WE ASK

Peace that flows like quiet waters
Lord, is all we ask
Joy to serve and joy to do
for every single task

Strength to live each single day
to count each blessing dear
with thankful heart to look to Thee
and freedom from all fear

Forgiveness Lord, if one should wrong
with humble heart we give
To always give that helping hand
We pray this life to live

And we ourselves know right from wrong
O teach us Lord we pray
to do our best with willing heart
to live this everyday

Not that we live for self alone
but others be our thought
O grant we ask, this humble prayer
Thy lessons we are taught

A CROSS

Each man in life must bear a cross
A burden we must bear
But what a joy to know that Christ
Our burdens He will share

To know that He is standing by
If we so humble ask
In love to fill our earthly needs
And strength for every task

And when the world seems dark without
There's always hope my friend
For Christ will hear if we but ask
A helping hand to lend

So if our Cross seems much at times
In Him, a privilege rare
To know that He, who's God Himself
For us that He should care

The burden of the Cross can be
Much less, if we but seek
His strength to share the load we bear
Lest we grow faint and weak.

LOST VALUES

I've known of some that's lost their way
Just live, not knowing why
Afraid to live, just marching time
And yet afraid to die.

They live today, just gathering dust
No purpose to their ways
They wake each morn, not caring much
To face another day

They search not for the good in life
No thanks for life to give
No joy to life, the goodness there
But just a task to live

They do not put much forth in life
And grasp what comes their way
To find such wrong in everything
and kind words never say

Just lost and wandering souls they
A wasted life to live
But how can one expect return
If one knows not to give

It takes much giving in this life
There's just no other way
Unselfish in our acts and deeds
Will steal our joys away

MEASURES

By some, I may not have so much
By others, seem a lot
But do we measure wealth alone
By things that's sold and bought

For instance, I, well, I can sleep
Nor trouble midst tonight
I have my sense of smell as well
And glad to have my sight

I have a job, perhaps not King
My needs are amply met
I cannot stake my all my life
In things that I may get.

I've never met a man as yet
If he based it all on gain
That lived to have just all he wants
To me, he lives in vain

Yes, I have far more than I need
Complaints I cannot give
For this would never give me joy
The purpose why I live

Roy V. Benson

FORGIVENESS

Forgiveness is the key to life
The key to joy and peace
for only then we'll find the good
and joys that never cease

Forgiveness of our fellow man
forgiveness from the heart
forgive and we well learn to find
that living really starts

Forgiving those that do us wrong
forgiving every day
for joy and peace and happiness
There is no other way

Forgiveness brings a heart of love
and love, a life that's true
and soon we learn to love each day
each day that comes anew

To live success, to make it right
Forgiveness is they key
As Christ forgave us in His love
Then goodness we shall see

GOD'S TOMORROW

In God's tomorrow yet to come
Where joys will never end
And sorrows be forever gone
Eternities to spend

No lonely hearts, nor fears assail
No sin in that fair land
Where darkness ne'er shall enter in
With Christ my King I'll stand

In God's tomorrow, O what joy
With Him to reign on high
In mansions there prepared for us
Where man will never die.

I live today, for God's tomorrow
I give Him thanks each day
For when I leave this earth below
I'm there with Him to stay.

Roy V. Benson

I MARVEL

Have you ever stood my friend
To marvel what you see
The trees so green and fields alike
Creation's plan so free

The pitter patter of the rain
It sings its own sweet song
You see my friend, I seem to know
Creation's plan belong

The flakes of snow that fall our way
They also serve so well
I like to think that every one
Another story tell

The sun with rays so warm and soft
Gives warmth to every man
Oh what a marvel this I see
Creation's master plan

The gentle winds, the rolling sea
The rivers and the dell
Each sings aloud, God's wondrous work
Creation's story tell

I like to stand in solemn praise
And marvel at His Hand
To give my thanks with humble heart
At God's creative plan.

LIFE

Would you take a walk with me
O'er trails that I have trod
O'er rocky paths, so bent and carved
O'er sun-baked fields of sod

O'er mountain tops to pause a bit
Enjoyment here to find
to live and leave forevermore
all trouble far behind.

If life would only grant to us
the days on mountains high
when life is good, to spread our wings
into the yonder sky.

But then there's days when down we go
in valleys dark and grim
to lift it seems so very hard
this victory to win.

So this is life, the paths we walk
each day there's something new
But if we try and pray for strength
our troubles seems so few.

Roy V. Benson

THE WHISPERS OF SUMMER

The summer breeze, so fresh, so warm
The specter of the trees
The flowers bursting forth about
It's such a sight to see

The birds, both old and young alike
sing praises through the day
to see the smile of folks we know
To hear the children play

The sunsets even bide their time
as nature sings with glee
It's all before my very eyes
And God has made it free

A WORD

A word is like a seed that's sown
it falls, we know not where
If sown in evil, then the fruit
It's evilness we share

A word in haste, or anger's tone
or gossip of a friend
No words can e'er undo the harm
This friendship ever mend

It'd pay for all to think once more
A word is like a seed
Would we enjoy this fruit to eat
Would we upon it feed?

So let us weigh each word we say
for someday they'll return
The fruits thereof will be the kind
The seeds e'er sown in turn.

Roy V. Benson

ONE DAY

One day I'll meet my Savior there
In starry skies above
I'm going home to be with Him
In His eternal love.

I know not when the hour may come
The trumpet blow on high
But Lord, I pray, to keep me close
To meet Thee in the sky

One day I'm going home at last
To leave this earth below
The hour or day it matters not
For surely Jesus knows

THE DAY'S END

The glow across the western sky
this day draws to an end
and what did I, in words or deeds
a helping hand to lend?

No more recapture, always gone
the minutes lost in tome
and did I live as I should live
were words and deeds most kind?

Was trust and faith that others place
in me, well guarded there
Did I take time to help that one
Another burdens share?

No more this day, the moments live
Be true in all I do
With words and deeds, be kind to call
These days that's all too few

Roy V. Benson

LIVING IN VAIN

It really doesn't matter much
The status we have gained
For if we live it just for self
We've lived it all in vain

It matters not how much we have
Of earthly goods and things
For if we had it all, we'd find
Such emptiness it'd bring

It's over, all so very soon
What have we really gained
These earthly goods to gather round
This life, to live in vain

THE WIND

I cannot see with open eyes
The wind that rushes madly by
It's sometimes fierce or just a sigh
And it seems at times to die.

But then it gathers force on high
It knows a whisper, knows a cry
For does it really ever die
This wind that rushes madly by.

I've looked away into the sky
And watched it push the clouds on high
I'll never know the where or why
Of wind that rushes madly by.

SOMEDAY

Someday I'm going home above
To glory land on high
no sorrows there, no lonely nights
no tears or hearts to cry.

I wonder what's prepared for me
In courts of Heavenly peace
such pleasures there, prepared above
Where joys will never cease
.

Such beauty rare, that never dies
A mansion there for me
to spend Eternal ages long
His glory there to see

Someday I'll go to glory land
and greet my Saviour there
He gave it all in wondrous love
His home on high to share

So friend if You should be there first
make room, I'm coming too
to that fair land, that home above
when this old life is through

RUNNING THE RACE

This life is but a race to run
I pray I run it well
I live, I must, as best I know
This life a story tells

My fellowman, I can't forget
of those about in need
for all I leave when I depart
are actions, words and deeds.

For when I leave this world behind
what words will others say
what trophies will I gather there
for all those earthly days?

Will others think in warmest tones
Will words be kindly said
for all those days I had below
for all those miles tread?

So I must run this race of life
I pray to run it well
That when I leave that others have
a kindly word to tell

Roy V. Benson

IT'S FUNNY WHAT MONEY WILL DO

What short loved friends we gather round
With things so gay and new
They know us well, these short lived friends
It's funny what money will do.

We'll get a pat, a bravo here
They know us well today
They'll surely be our friends for life
It's funny what money will do

Then as the days grow into years
Our health and gaiety gone
And wealth eludes in days gone past
It's funny what money will do

And if we lose what has been ours
These friends no more be found
They've gone to other pastures green
It's funny what money will do

It can divide a family tree
To hate and bitter strife
Where each would want the others to share
It's funny what money will do

It happens all around us friend
The things that money can buy
From real joys to bitter hate
It's funny what money will do

When all the chips have fallen hard
When wealth should be no more
Then count your friends, you'll come up short
It's funny what money will do

Oh yes, your friends have all but ceased
The days grow long and drear
No longer does the laughter ring
It's funny what money will do

Roy V. Benson

HE HOLDS THE ANSWERS

He holds the answers in His hands
My Lord knows every need
Desires of the heart of man
In pastures green He leads

He know the sorrows, know the tears
He knows the joys as well
He knows what lies ahead each day
He know it all so well

So if I trust my Lord to guide
and live within His love
He'll steer my life on earth below
and guide it from above

So Lord, I pray, do take command
forgive, when I fail Thee
and make me better Lord each day
Thy goodness I will see

WHAT IF

What if the Lord in haste had left
The color out of trees
What beauty would we look upon
What beauty would we see?

What if the grass were colorless
and snowflakes never white
and crocuses would never close
their eyes throughout the night?

What if a rose knew color not
and daffodils as well
what beauty would a rose display
what story would they tell?

What if the skies were colorless
No crimson splendor there
the clouds no white, the skies no blue
would skies be then called fair?

Or ocean waters were without
a color there to see
I wonder how we'd look upon
what beauty would there be?

But oh to think of birds so small
no color in their wings
I wonder how they'd sound to us
If birds they could not sing?

Just think if He'd in haste forgot
to add the color fair
what would we look with eyes upon
what beauty would we share?

Roy V. Benson

No, I for one, give him humble thanks
He planned it all so well
for everywhere I look about
His love for us he tells

MY PRAYER AT BEDTIME

I lay me down to sleep, my Lord
a pleasant rest I pray
and keep my soul, my all in Thee
Until the break of day.

I pray no troubled thoughts within
No worries play their part
and if I live to see the morn
That day with joy to start.

O help me Lord, through everyday
each day Thou grants to me
that I may do my best in all
Each day, its goodness see

So as I lay me down to sleep
I ask this Lord to be
to grant me faith, to know these things
Be safely held by Thee

Roy V. Benson

A PATTERN I BE

If I thought a precious child
were watching all my ways
would I live and do those things
that I have done today?

Would I say the words I said
those places would I go
The deeds, are they all right for him
The living that I show?

I wonder if my tones would change
if he should pattern me
would I look when he's a man
Be proud, the things I see?

If he followed in my steps
could he, by weakness fall
Be doing just what I have done
if He should give his all?

Am I the man that I should be
if one should pattern me
and walk and live as I do live
What would this child be?

I pray I never fail a child
If I should be that one
to have him walk in steps I've walked
when this old life is done

IF I HAD

If I had the worlds wealth
it's precious gems and stones
What would I have if this were mine
to feel myself alone?

If I lived in mansions fair
Commands were mine to give
Would I have very much
a life of ease to live?

If I had these earthly things
but yet no one to care
Would I count it all in vain
My love, no one to share?

I have learned the real wealth
The things that have the worth
are not the gems, the rubies fair
material things of earth.

The real wealth is to be found
in others that we know
a neighbor, friend, or sweetheart dear
the kindness that we show

In trust and faith, in love itself
in doing, nor for self
for these alone will give more joy
than all the world's wealth.

Roy V. Benson

"REACH OUT, REACH OUT"

"Reach out, reach out," I yelled aloud
"there overhead, a hanging bough"
and there upon he raised his hand
to grasp the bough thrust forth from land.

He looked above and said these words
the saddest words I've ever heard
Thanks God, but now I can take o'er
I really don't need you no more

At once the branch gave way and then
I saw no more where once he's been
The thought he could now do his way
He was so close yet swept away.

And so it seems, we live this way
We'll call on God another day
But when we're swept from solid ground
I pray that then the bough be found

I pray the floods of life be kind
and be they not, a bough to find
but look above my God to thee
and may I ever grateful be.

GIVING OF SELF

What thought do we plant, what seeds do we sow
for these will determine, a child as it grows
how much do we keep or how much do we give
or think of ourselves, each day that we live?

The things that will count, are deeper than gold
Love can't be bought, nor can it be sold
it's deeper than all, more precious than time
The more that we give, the more we will find.

If we would but learn, the more that we give
each day that we have is richer to live
for giving of self, is love that is true
How much do we give, how much do we do?

Roy V. Benson

WORDS THAT WE SOW

Words that are spoken in anger and haste
They're not left to die or just go to waste
A seed that is planted to grow as it may
The fruit from that seed, will be a harvest someday

What fruit will we harvest, what harvest we gain
who is to blame, if we harvest in vain
a finger of guilt, whom shall we say
We reap what we sow, there's no other way.

Remember that words are seeds of the day
let us sow them in love, each word let us weigh
words are but seeds, let us sow them with care
let us carefully plan, good harvests to bear.

A NEW DAY

This day is new, not lived before
I wonder what it holds in store
What shall I do with all this time
or shall I say, "I'll call it mine."

Each morn I wake do I complain
as though it's lost and naught to gain
as though the sun will not shine through
and joys I see are all too few?

Ungrateful souls, a chance to live
But how much living do we give
to make another soul to smile
will we walk that extra mile?

Oh let us look upon each day
in hope and love, in kindly ways
and give our thanks that we may live
some other soul, our joy to give.

For we will give unto this day
just how we feel along the way
a day of waste, or day of gain
Oh let us smile and not complain

Roy V. Benson

O FOOLISH MAN

Oh foolish man with sight so small
Why does thou fight and fume
O'er things that have no real wealth
and vanish all too soon?

Thy barns are full, thou wealth dost flow
and yet thou wantest more
a friend you'll tread, a loved one too
more wealth thou hast to store.

There is no end to greed my friend
thy thirst shall burn thee up
for when thou gettest thou wants more
to fill thy greedy cup.

But then it all will end too soon
thy life be lived in vain
a few short years on earth below
no thought of Heaven's gain

Before the Judgment seat of God
what wilt thou have to say
"I lived, my God, for self alone
I lived for me each day"

Oh foolish man to think of "me"
as others though have trod
no thought of love and kindness sow
a wretched life thou's bought

My friend we'll all stand at the door
the Judgment seat to face
It's not the wealth that we have gained
but how we've run the race.

You'd better think and change thy ways
for life on earth is short
for all mankind, be big or small
Be judged in Heaven's Court.

Roy V. Benson

TONIGHT AND TOMORROW

I love to see the shadows fall
As evening time draws nigh
to see the sun as it goes down
into the western sky.

And soon I'll lay me down to rest
My thanks my Lord I'll give
for having had the privilege great
this day for me to live.

Now as I slumber through the night
If I should wake, I pray
to give my thanks for all those things
the blessings of each day

Oh give me strength tomorrow Lord
do better than today
In acts and deeds where I walk
in words that I may say.

And now I close my eyes to sleep
another day is through
and if I wake what joy to find
another day so new.

IT DOESN'T BELONG TO YOU

What makes you think, a claim you have
on something you've not earned
you have no claim, it isn't yours
this selfish man you've turned

You've had no sweat, no tails there
and yet you think it's yours
You'll walk on friend and loved one too
to gain a little more

It doesn't really belong to you
you greedy grasping one
but yet you'll walk on other men
to gain that paltry sum

No joy, no peace, shall be your fare
You've gained your selfish end
your lot in life, I pity then
a foolish man my friend.

SAY SON

"Say Son, where goest thou my friend
With heart so proud and true."
"I goest, Dad, into the world
In search of something new."

"I ask thee son, to guard thy ways
Be careful, lest ye fall
I'll always keep a listening ear
To hear ye if ye call."

Remember Son, the pitfalls there
Be strong in all ye do
Look up and ask His guiding Hand
In turn, thy trials be few

Be honest, brave, in all be true
Thy mark, I pray thee make
Return my son, that I for one
Thy hand, with pride may shake

"Good-bye my dad, Thou taught me well
I'll fear not any test
I'll ask for strength, to guide me well
In each, to do my best."

As Dad, I'll ask with humble heart
My son, be brave and strong
As he goes out to venture forth
His days on earth be long.

O LORD, I ASK

O Lord I ask of You my God
To keep me straight and strong
To keep me on the narrow road
To keep me from all wrong.

O Lord I ask of You my God
To open all my doors
To light the paths that I should tread
To know Thee only more

O Lord I ask of You my God
To take me by thy Hand
To make me good and just and true
With strength, that I may stand.

O Lord I ask of You my God
Forgive, when I am weak
For Lord you see, I only want
The Love is what I seek.

Roy V. Benson

AUTUMN TIME

What makes the sun so brilliant red
Against the clouds so white
The beauty of a setting sun
As it goes out of sight?

What makes the moon a ball of fire
O'er yonder hill away
To hang as though suspended there
At the ending of the day?

What makes the leaves of autumn turn
To herald the summer's end
The trees turn bare to close their eyes
In sleep, the winter spend?

What makes the darkness gather fast
And shadows cast their spell
To dance on breath of autumn time
Each one a story tell?

What makes the birds seek homes so snug
Their songs not quite so gay
And little creatures of the woods
A place their heads to lay?

What makes the summer yield to fall
No more, the trees so green
And everywhere that I should look
A changing nature scene?

It's planned so well by God above
Each season serves so well
And beauty rare to everyone
The seasons four to tell

I'm glad He gave in love so free
The wondrous autumn time
Such beauty there for all to see
Such beauty there to find.

Roy V. Benson

OUR HOME ON HIGH

O'er yonder skies, beyond in space
A lovely home, a lovely place
Prepared on high for you and me
Our home on high eternally

Where streets are paved of solid gold
And man will never there grow old
No heartaches, trials or tears be there
In Heaven's glory land so fair

It's all well worth it, dearest friend
Your life on earth for Christ to spend
For life is but a vapor here
And Heaven's presence O so near.

So let us set our sights on high
To that fair home beyond the skies
For wonders there will never cease
Where troubled hearts will know God's peace.

A MAN OF MUCH WEALTH I HAVE ENOUGH

I have food in the cupboard and clothes on my back
My house is much better than many a shack
A job that perhaps doesn't give me much wealth
But nevertheless, I do have my health.

My bills I can pay, even though it is tough
You know I am thinking, I don't have it rough
Oh, many a thing, I would want for myself
But many a thing would just lie on the shelf

The shoes on my feet aren't expensive and gay
But they get me there, if I lead the way.
My legs at least work, my body propel
I'm certainly rich, I'm healthy and well.

There's certainly something in which to complain
perhaps it is this, that I can't see much gain
but when would I feel, each want would be met
That thirst can't be quenched, I'm willing to bet.

You know I don't think I have it so bad
There's many a reason for me to be glad
My home and my job, my health and my wife
I really don't have that bad of a life.

So this very day, I think I will say
be thankful that I can pay my own way
be thankful for this as well as my health
consider myself a man of much wealth.

Roy V. Benson

STEPPING STONES

This life is but a stepping stone
to greater things above
for those that seek the Saviour's will
For those that seek His love

A stepping stone for that beyond
Eternities ahead
Where will you spend those ages long
Where will your soul be led?

It's up to you, no other one
The choice is yours alone
For then it be too late, my friend
Before that Great White Throne

I pray you heed the Saviour's voice
Repent, Be saved today
This is the only way to Christ
There is no other way.

THE VOYAGE OF LIFE

Life is a like a voyage, Lord
On seas we set our sails
We must make port, our home above
or then we only fail

The storms of life can rock the ship
This voyage that I sail
So Lord, I pray to keep me close
In storms, I will not fail

And then we see the lights on shore
we've made the harbor there
our voyage ends, we're home at last
Thy glorifies then to share

Roy V. Benson

THE FAUCETS OF HEAVEN

I like the way the Lord doth things
It always seem just right
He gave the day when man should work
And rest, the hours of night

I like to think of gentle rains
On garden walls that fall
And hear the wind in restless tones
Or birds, their mates to call

The leaves that turn from green to red
As nature goes to sleep
I need not hear, they will not wake
For God, their beauty keeps

I really have to say I like
The way He doeth things
For everything my Father does
Such beauty does it bring

YOUR WILL

God gave to all a human will
entrusted in your care
It's yours to do, it's yours alone
your will, no man can share

This will of yours will make the rules
your paths will lie ahead
your will will make it all for you
that portion be your bed

Are you so strong to walk alone
you need a guiding hand
Be certain friend, lest you should fall
your will will help you stand?

O treat it kind, this will of yours
Entrusted in your care
Be careful friend, for evil lurks
Be strong, lest temptress snare

Roy V. Benson

GRIND ON

This world turns on, it grinds away
with evil, lust and fear
oh every hand such human greed
its presence ever near

"More" we cry, O give us more
our thirst grows greater still
What matter if on those we tread
our greedy nature fill

O face it man, in all your pomp
Decay be yours too soon
the paths you walk, your heap ahead
will lie in rack and ruin

Your greed will grind you up in waste
the heap grows larger still
and yet they cry, "O give us more"
each storehouse that they fill

Now let me ask you this my friend
will joy be yours to share
will love and goodness follow you
with strength for trials to bear?

O think my friend, the world turns on
what portion can you claim
It's up to you to make the rules
It's how you play the game?

Grind on, grind on, you'll gain your end
you'll reap the harvest sown
and none will hear, as you cry out
"If I had only known"

AWAY BEYOND

I'm looking friend, away beyond
away beyond the blue
Look there my friend, way out beyond
The home I'm going to.

It's really something, friend, I know
with Angels, streets of gold
I've only seen a sketchy glimpse
as in the Bible told.

Just imagine, no more night
in this great glory land
and friend, a tree, the tree of life
and joy on every hand.

Oh friend, just look away beyond
it's there, in yonder blue
This home of beauty, rare delight
when this old life is through

Roy V. Benson

I WON'T TELL THEM

They'll never know the hurt they caused
They'll never know the love that's lost
They'll never know emotions cost
They'll never know, I won't tell them

They'll never know the tears were shed
They'll never know the heart that bled
They'll never know those words they said
They'll never know, I won't tell them

They'll never know the reasons why
They'll never know that grown men cry
They'll never know and they won't try
They'll never know, I won't tell them

They'll never know and why should they
They'll never know it's just their way
They'll never know these things I say
They'll never know, I won't tell them

MY SOUL

It matters not what you may do
You cannot hurt my soul
The hurts and arrows shot my way
It's true, they take their toll

What words you use in courts of law
What hurt you heap on me
You never can destroy my soul
FOREVER MINE TO KEEP

Accusing words, each word you said
Each word, a seed was sown
You're probably thinking now my friend
"if I had only known"

My soul is mine alone to keep
Off limits to you friend
For it's committed to my God
Until the very end

Destroy at will what e'er you want
Accuse me what you may
But always will my Soul live on
It's God's, with Him to stay.

Roy V. Benson

YOU'LL NEVER KNOW

You'll never know the hurt that you give
You'll never know the hurt that I live
You'll never know the crying inside
You'll never know the tears that I hide

You'll never know the wounds that I felt
You'll never know the scars they have dealt
You'll never know how long be the nights
You'll never know they're hidden from sight

You'll never know the dreams torn apart
You'll never know the dream had its start
You'll never know the love you have tread
You'll never know the hurt you have said

You'll never know it's better this way
You'll never know in living each day
You'll never know they're now of the past
You'll never know how long they will last

You'll never know, oh what a shame
You'll never know playing your game
You'll never know it's over and done
And not I must wonder, who really won

DOT YOUR I'S

What hurt we give our fellowman
What arrows shoot his way
For anything that he does wrong
We'll surely make him pay

"Dot your I's and cross your T's"
Each word you'd better weigh
For if you don't remember friend
We're here to make you pay

It matters not just who we tread
What words in haste we say
We're certain what we want to do
We want the man to pay

Be careful, lest some man will think
"I Thought I heard you say"
For speaking you offend someone
This man will make you pay

Oh what a world we have become
When every word we weigh
To dot your I's and cross your T's
Just so we needn't pay

What is the outcome of this life
What hope for better days
When one must hide from other men
Just so he doesn't pay

CRITICAL

Critical people in
Critical ways
Critical in the
things that they say

Critical of
the things that they see
Critical of
the things that may be

Critical of
the things that go wrong
Critical of
the fact that they belong

Critical is
and always will be
Critical for
others to see

WOUNDED SOUL

I've been a wounded soul at times
And justly, you may say
Perhaps I earned the hurt received
Perhaps the piper pay

I've kept these wounds within myself
No others really care
They have their wounds as well, my friend
They have their cross to bear

So some may be well justified
While others did not earn
But if I look within that wound
A lesson there to learn

So do we try to hurt because
A wounded man inside
Perhaps we cannot really show
These feelings cannot hide

So every soul a wound to heal
A cross we all must bear
Each wound will heal but leave a scar
Each soul, a burden bear

Roy V. Benson

BLINDED EYES

Satan blinds the eyes of men
Complete the blindness be
No longer do they know what's right
The wrong, they cannot see

Blinded eyes, they're all around
They do not count the cost
And never do they realize
The good that they have lost

Oh what a pity this should be
The wrongs, they now call right
You wonder if they ever will
Regain their stolen sight

These blinded eyes no longer see
It really is a shame
One wonders if they'll turn around
And things might be the same

Be careful lest this Satan blinds
He does, so cleverly
It's all his plan to close your eyes
For sin, you will not see

IF I EARNED THEM

I guess I've earned the hurt I get
The arrows shot my way
Perhaps they really want to get
To really make me pay

They make it look as bad I am
The words they use on me
They use these words in printed form
with no apology

I wonder if these words be meant
These words of hurt they say
And yet be meant, they surely must
To hurt a soul this way

So if I've earned these words of hurt
The arrows shot my way
I cannot blame another soul
For things that I must pay

So if I've earned them let me pay
no malice towards that one
For we must pay our wrongs in life
For things we've said and done

Roy V. Benson

IN THE MIDST

In the midst of turmoil and grief
The house seem so long in a day
If only you'd look to Heaven above
He's only a prayer away.

In the midst of the tears that you shed
Your heart grows heavy with pain
if only you'd look to Heaven above
the Courts of Heaven you'd gain

In the midst of troubles on earth
It seems, no answers you know
If only you'd look to Heaven above
His love, to you He would show

In the midst of all of these things
Give thanks for Christ know them all
If only you'd look to Heaven above
No problem's too large or too small

In the midst have patience my friend
No way is God shadowed by time
If humbly you ask, you'll humbly receive
the patience, you surely will find

OWNERSHIP

What makes you think these things are yours
The earth, the land and sea
They're only loaned a little while
They're loaned to you and me

You think that deeds may say they're yours
It does, but brief the time
for you will have to give them up
another man will find

The things you count so precious now
will one day slip away
and you will no more own these things
there is no other way

So own, I wonder if you do?
afraid you don't my friend
for if you owned you'd take them with
and there would be no end

Oh foolish man cling to those things
Your barns fill selfishly
Remember though, the day will come
you'll face Eternity

So barns that filled to overflow
just now, what good are they
if only you had one more chance
You'd lived another way

You'd better think, what is their worth
what future do you see?
We all must stand before our God
When then the owner be?

Roy V. Benson

Do give some thought before too late
the values, Are they true?
remember they're not really yours
they're only loaned to you

So everything must have a cost
what cost put on your Soul?
for if I'm right and you should lose
You've paid a heavy toll

LOOKING BACK

I'll never live this life again
I must look back to when
I wonder what when I look back
The things I'll see my friend

Will they be good when we look back
These things be proud to see
I wonder what, it makes one think
That day, our thoughts will be

I do believe each man will have
to see, in retrospect
and we must surely realize
the things we can expect

Never will I live this life
again, to pass this way
I guess I'd better make it count
and do some good today

Roy V. Benson

PURPOSE

What is your purpose here on earth
Why do you really live
Is it for self to feed upon
Or live your life to give

Do you take all that you can get
Your nest, to feather well
Your life shows up as neon lights
A story there to tell

What purpose is this life of yours
What purpose here on earth
What value do you put on things
What value is their worth?

A question we must ask ourselves
Just what we're doing here
Our answers come up short, my friend
Far short, I really fear.

ACCOMPLISHMENTS SO FEW

How great we are or so we think
our lives we glorify
we build momentous unto self
as though they'd never die

We do not want the world forget
How great we really are
Momentous great for all to see
Our great and shining star

"Oh notice me, I am so great
the things I've done and said"
and yet they're gone, forgotten then
soon after we are dead

So foolish man, what have you gained
what glories liveth on
I'll tell you friend, they're all in vain
The day that you are gone

So boast and build how great you are
A foolish man are you
For all will turn to grains of sand
Accomplishments so few

So what may be your goal on earth
To boast how great you are?
to show this world that it may know
this great and shining star

It matter not the day you die
How great or what you've done
it only counts when life is o'er
the race that you have run

89

Roy V. Benson

I know a way eternally
Accomplishments live on
it's only if forget thyself
and join the Christian throne.

DISTORTED VIEWS

Distorted views, of life we get
Our thought go far astray
We live to gather unto self
We live unto this day

These things of earth consume our thoughts
The need we think so great
We'd do most anything to get
For things we cannot wait

But all in vain to fill our lives
Such vanity we live
These things of earth so quickly gone
What pleasure did they give?

So back to dust and rust they go
for time will take its toll
for all these things that you must have
With time grows old

All these things of earth you have
these things you value great
will someday tumble round your feet
and then it be too late

So gather well, your thoughts my friend
Your values, what their worth
these things my friend, you treasure in
are only of this earth

So set your values on a plain
Eternal Godly things
on things that live forevermore
true happiness will bring

Roy V. Benson

IF I

If I owned the world itself
its gems and precious stones
what value there, what would I have
If I were all alone?

If I had such riches vast
or say just moderate wealth
what would I have if all alone
to spend it on myself?

If I could have the finest things
that wealth itself could buy
What joy to find what pleasures there
if here my heart should cry

No, I have found that there's much more
than wealth and earthly things
to make a song, to give a heart
a song of joy to sing.

RUN, IF YOU CAN

Millions are hurting about us is life
with hunger and pain and cold
what are you doing, your brother to help
as repeatedly this story is told

It'd hurt my friend no place for your head
Your body cries but for a meal
You surely must hear, the cry of the poor
Somehow, this agony feel

In all of your comfort, snug as you are
How can you turn him aside
It won't go away, your mind to erase
And no where that you can hide.

So those of us have, must give of our means
Our blessing be willing to share
It's expected of us by Jesus above
to show in His Love that we care

Roy V. Benson

YOUR CONSCIENCE

Going north, going south
Going east or west
You'll never leave it far behind
Your conscience never rest

Running here, running there
Running to and from
You'll never run away from it
Your conscience always know

Money here, money there
Money cannot buy
So if your conscience bothers you
You know the reason why

Pleasures now, pleasure then
Pleasures cannot hide
For in the midst of all if this
Your conscience at your side

So run or walk, try to hide
You'll never make it friend
For conscience is a part of you
It's with you till the end

So game of life, play it straight
Your conscience be your guide
The cleaner that you play the game
The less you have to hide

CALENDAR OF TIME

The calendar of time displays
Just where in time we be
From many happenings in this world
The many things we see

The wars and riots all about
No trust in fellowman
It just about will tell the time
In History, we stand

Dishonesty and theft prevails
A man will steal his share
No more disgrace should he get caught
And no one really cares

Hunger rules In many lands
Food in short supply
It seems that man has closed his ear
To other men that cry

Our pleasures, sports and selfish gain
It rules our very being
We're quick to turn the other way
From things we may be seeing

We're certain that we must come first
It's ours to have and hold
Our minds are quick to close them off
These things that we are told

"So cry you world, I've got Mine"
It's what we seem to say
"We do not have the time to give
Perhaps another day."

Roy V. Benson

So wars and self and sin abounds
No limits does it know
I think the hour is closing in
The midnight hour shows

The calendar of time is told
In all these many things
I wonder when the hand will move
To strike the final ring

EACH TRIAL

Each trial that we have
New strength to attain
I pray only Lord
A victory to gain

Each trial that we have
The hurt that we live
Our strength be in God
In strength that He gives

So give me the strength
My Lord now I pray
For each of these trials
That cometh my way

Weakness be mine
But strength may I ask
Do help me my Lord
Live up to the task

So strength will I seek
For trials of this day
I trust in the Lord
To show me the way

Roy V. Benson

LAWYER'S JUNGLE

A lawyer's jungle soon will be
From now until eternity
This way of life is here to stay
And man will know no other way

Each man will sue the other one
Some be lost and some be won
The lawyers gather in their gain
As suing soon becomes sour game

A complex world will see these things
For every suit, another brings
A way of life is here to stay
As we will make the other pay

A lawyer's jungle, what a shame
Survival means to play the game
I hope I'm wrong, but oh friend
It's here to stay until the end

So careful be lest you get sued
Not always what you say or do
It's just a way of life today
Another person makes you pay

It's such a shame that this is life
It adds unto the daily strife
As each man seeks to gain for self
Will even take another's wealth

So sue you must, the lawyer's creed
Just let him talk he'll plant the seed
And you will gain another's wealth
Ill-gotten gains unto yourself

A lawyer's jungle, yes my friend
A lawyer's jungle knows no end
So careful lest the words you say
Another man will make you pay

HUNGER

The problems of this world are great
they've really just begun
They really can't be solved by man
Not solved by anyone

Just take the case of food alone
It gains by one by two by three
It cannot do the job too well
This gain's too small you see

Now people gain by two by four
by eight and greater still
how can this food be multiplied
the needs of people fill

It's bigger than the minds of men
This problem of mankind
I really think they don't know how
Solutions there to find

So problems yes, I mention one
Just one, of many more
I wonder what the future holds
Just what it has in store

You see, my friend, that hunger can
Drive men to do weird things
The world will see just what they are
These things that hunger brings

How soon that day, I do not know
It's certain to arrive
for hunger drives a man beyond
He'll die to stay alive.

THE SIREN

The siren screams its woeful tune
there's trouble of some kind
It's destined to seek out, my friend
The trouble it will find

A woeful time, played far too much
each day we hear it more
I'm glad I don't know every time
just what it's screaming for

A troubled call it answers then
A soul, be hurting there
I guess the siren really says
"Hold on, we really care"

a woeful tune, but yet a song
a song that someone cares
the siren sings "We're on our way"
to help a soul out there

So think not of the woeful side
but think of mercy kind
and then a different tune you'll hear
A different sound you'll find

LONELY

Lonely hours and lonely days
Lonely people lonely ways
Lonely in their thoughts as well
Lonely yes, but never tell

Lonely hours in lonely nights
waiting for the break of light
Lonely and afraid to dream
Just too lonely, it would seem

Lonely homes with lonely rooms
Lonely only seems their doom
Lonely every hour each day
Lonely seems their only way

Lonely hearts with lonely tears
Lonely hearts we do not hear
Lonely souls be all around
Lonely souls that make no sound

Lonely souls weep deep inside
Lonely souls their tears they hide
Lonely, you may never know
Lonely, does not always show

Lonely knows no where to hide
for the hurt goes deep inside
Lonely smiles amongst the tears
Lonely's presence ever near

Lonely souls cannot extend
hands to reach out to a friend
we may never really know
Lonesome souls not always show

Lonely Soul if I should meet
help me Lord, this soul to greet
help me in the things I say
Lonely Soul, turn not away

COMPATIBLE

Compatible folks in
Compatible ways
Compatible in
the things we may say

Compatible thoughts
with compatible deeds
Compatible friends
with compatible needs

Compatible husbands
with compatible wives
Compatible homes
with compatible lives

Compatible with
all nature we see
Compatible may
our lives ever be

Compatible faith
with compatible love
Compatible hopes
anchored above.

EACH DAY

Each day that we have
Is one less that we live
We only receive
The days that He gives

We're promised each one
allotted a time
we know not the day
or tomorrow we find

Each morning give thanks
each morning you see
no man knows the days
what day this may be

Each day that we live
has shortened our stay
be thankful my friend
for each Blessed day

Allotted a time
no lengthening the stay
Lift up your heads
Give Thanks for the day

I THANK THEE

I thank Thee, Lord, for years gone by
The many days I've had
for home, for love and children songs
to hear their voices glad.

I thank Thee, Lord, for all the things
In love, Thou gave to me
such goodness Lord, I know it well
can only come from Thee

I thank Thee, Lord, what lies ahead
My footsteps thou wilt guide
But Lord, I thank Thee most of all
for me, my sins, thou died

I thank Thee, Lord, my prayer to hear
To know that Thou doest care
To know I journey not alone
My burden Thou doest bear

TO MY DAUGHTER

My daughter dear, I say in love
this little thing I say
Be kind and good to those about
you meet along life's way

O learn to look for good in all
there's good in all mankind
Your life will then be full of joy
such pleasure you will find

So daughter dear, I love so much
You've been a joy to me
for when I look into your life
such goodness do I see

I'm thankful for each day I've had
to love you as my own
I thank you dear for all the times
the love to me you've shown

Roy V. Benson

THE SHOE

There has been those been on the take
to take most what they could
they'd gather all to feed themselves
Perhaps they thought they should

I guess they thought the more they have
then happy they would be
it matter not the hurt that's done
it's only self they see

To fill their barns that they may have
'Tis all they really know
what souls they tread along the way
they trust will never show

But yet this void cannot be filled
their efforts be in vain
but oh they plot in evil ways
more things that they may gain

To give perhaps, a pittance here
they do for conscience sake
they'll never change, they don't know how
for self, they're on the take

So if the shoe should fit you well
then wear it my dear friend
this shoe will always be so near
you'll wear it to the end.

THE FINEST

The finest hotels, the finest in town
The finest jewels, and furs to be found
The finest you want, your ego to feed
The finest supplies, your selfish needs

The finest be yours, so certain you be
The finest be yours, for other to see
The finest be yours, it's life at its best
The finest be yours, too bad for the rest

The finest in cars, play things galore
The finest in clothes, you only want more
The finest is yours, you jealously claim
The finest is yours, it's part of your game

The finest you have, the finest is yours
The finest in life, you're living for
The finest be gone, in such short of time
The finest has lost, My friend, you will find

The finest will end, the years will close in
The finest has bought, what God would call sin
The finest you had, now what be the cost
The finest was yours, but a Soul be the loss.

Roy V. Benson

5 YEARS FORWARD AND 3 YEARS BACK

5 years forward and 3 years back
oh how they scramble to cover their tracks
the lives that they scatter, the hurt that they cause
they're only concerned to cover their loss

The trick of the trade some taxes to gain
I really don't know the rules of the game
But there is a way the cards that are stacked
5 years forward and 3 years back

They count not the cost and nor do they care
the rules of the game are not very fair
remember my friend, this is a fact
it's 5 years forward and 3 years back

RIOTS AND WARS

There's certainly talk of riot and wars
I know it's gone on for centuries before
But when will man learn that greed does not pay
Is this all man knows, in his civilized way?

A reason they find, why these things must be
Perhaps they may say, "to set someone free"
But I wonder if, the profits were bare
If men held in power, this freedom would care?

I wonder how long these countries will fight
certainly each country, must think it is right
so all I can see is more riots and wars
It's certainly great, what man has in store

Money and profit, wars fought in greed
a more token payment, some hunger to feed
the needs of the world are not important, I guess
while profits and greed keep the world in a mess

Roy V. Benson

THE EQUALIZER

Great big homes and fancy cars
Trips to everywhere
Boats and planes, the better things
Life without a care

Wardrobes full of fancy clothes
Charge accounts galore
Stocks and bonds, bank note too
These things we're living for

Jet set condos, foreign shores
Fashion shows as well
Money flows, we gather in
Each thing we buy or sell

Paris fashions, polo shows
Parties here and there
A life of ease our portion be
A life without a care

But then the equalizer comes
Death, we know its name
We cannot take a thing with us
In death, we're all the same

All these things we counted great
This day, be all in vain
What lies ahead this unknown path
What then will be our gain?

And in the shadows there he stands
The equalizer waits
And no man knows just how to void
In keeping with this date

The equalizer can't be bought
By all your jewels so fair
I wonder then what will you think
What then will be your share?

So fancy clothes and jet set styles
What then will be your cost
For you will stand before the Judge
To find that you have lost

I can't imagine why some think
It's theirs to have and hold
And they will never change their mind
They never can be told

Good-bye my friend, you live your life
You live it as you see
Know well the equalizer comes
What then your portion be?

Roy V. Benson

GIVING AND TAKING

What is your desire, this life that you live
To take all you want with nothing to give
To feed inner self and others forget
To selfishly gather all you can get?

To feed inner man in your selfish way
To gain all you can, this game that you play
And when is enough, the want be no more
What in the world, your life hold in store

These things of this earth, will grow weary and old
These things that you treasure, grow dreary and cold
You've gathered to self all of these years
These things that you foolishly counted so dear

If wiser you'd been and shared of your goods
If only you'd given, those days that you could
But now you are set, to give, there's no room
Now that your life, this greed has consumed

So giving and taking, a pattern is set
Some men will take all they can get
But thanks be to God, that others will give
Others will give so that others can live

For all have a choice, to give or take
To live for ourselves and others forsake
To live with our blessings with others to share
To live with our blessings with others to care

So treasures laid up in God's Heaven beyond
Will dividends pay those eternities long
But things of this earth be ever short lived
It's all up to you to take or to give.

GIVE THEM ONE

Give them one, and they'll want two
Two, and they'll want four
they'll reach and reach and only want
their greed will ask for more

Their greed can never satisfy
their wants, they think they need
their hunger grows, beyond all hope
This appetite they feed

So give them one and you will find
that two becomes their share
for now consumed in selfish gain
for self they only care

I've seen it time and time again
I'm sure you have, my friend
for greed will take them to their grave
It stays until the end.

O take your one or make it two
or maybe three or four
you'll never change, you've set your course
of greed forevermore

Roy V. Benson

PENNY PINCHERS

Some people think, I do believe
They'll never leave this earth
They pinch and scrape each penny dear
And only count their worth

Their blessings they are blind to see
They think it all is theirs
They cannot give with open heart
With others, gifts to share.

The more they have, the more they want
Their thirst just grows and grows
There is no end to human greed
This selfishness they show

But what will happen on that day
An account, we'll have to give
I'm sure we'll wish it could be changed
This life on earth we lived.

What is your life, and is it all
you'd like to have my friend
for this life is o'er and gone
Where then your life to spend

So think and pray this very day
before it be too late
Will you be standing there without
at Heaven's pearly gates.

THE AUCTIONEER

"For sale, for sale," cries the auctioneer
"This soul," he telleth the crowd
"How much is your bid, what may it be worth?"
as the bidding gets noisy and loud

"For sale, for sale, who'll bid up this soul.
Come, let the bidding be lively and gay.
For here is a man, that's taken a stand
His soul, he'll sell for this day."

Isn't it strange, how a dollar to gain
our soul, we'll sell long the way
we seem to care not, the devil has bought
our soul, as we live for the day.

Be careful my friend, lest your soul it be bid
A paltry sum but to gain
For what you have lost, a pity my friend
this life, will have been lived in vain.

A LOWLY BID

"Goin' once, goin' twice,
A lowly Bid" he cried
But no one raised the bid that day
no matter how he tried

No worth put on this soul to die
The world has had its way
He lived as though he'd never see
His last and dying day.

The pleasures of this earth fade fast
They're here for but a time
Then who'll be there to bid your soul
Which auctioneer you'll find.

"A lowly Bid" your lot be cast
or will the worth be great
you are the one to make the choice
You're master of your fate

There's only two to auction in
Your Soul. And who'll it be
The Devil or My Christ, the King
My friend, it's up to thee

THAT WILL

I'm sure that those who die and leave
A trust, for those behind
Would really wonder if it's worth
these things we really find

I wonder if these things are worth
the hate and greed they bring
for all have changed, each person then
a different tune to sing

We point our fingers at that one
We never are to blame
We never stop one time to think
of all the things we've gained

Divided families, friends won't speak
We want our very share
the chips may fall, it matters not
and no one seems to care

Disgusting, yes, it really is
afraid someone will gain
a little more that we may get
"a dirty rotten shame."

So those that die, they mean quite well
but little do they know
what greed and lust and selfishness
can sometime really show

We fight as though we worked so hard
We fight as though we earned
each penny given in this will
when will we ever learn

ILL-GOTTEN GAINS

Sue them high, or sue them low
Sue them fast or sue them slow
Sue them now or sue them then
Sue them each, foe or friend

So sue them all, it's vogue today
to some they gain, it is a way
The gain they get, lights up their eyes
They think it's smart, they think it's wise

So sue is in, the lawyer's laugh
another soul will get the shaft
so sue him high or sue them low
"We'll bleed him dry, he'll never know"

A way of life, we've now proclaimed
Another suit, another name
We've joined the ranks of sue, sue, sue
Be sure to get what's coming to you

But little friend, I've news for you
Those paltry bucks will be too few
For dollars gained in such a way
will last you such a few short days

Ill-gotten gains will disappear
You'll rue the day, I truly fear
And if you could go back and change
Ill-gotten gains, are all in vain

THE EVIL MIND

What evil lurks in minds of men
In evilness they plan
if only we could turn around
this evilness of man

They come in clothing of a sheep
But friend, do not be fooled
for they are trained in evil ways
in evil, they are schooled

Their charm is great, convincing words
they know their game plan well
But deep within a story's told
another story tell

So evil men plot evil moves
they think In evil ways
so think it out and guard your tongue
in things you do and say

Roy V. Benson

THE MIGHTY PEN

Destruction with the mighty pen
Destruction of a soul
Destruction great and swift as well
The Pen can take its toll

We tear that soul in ragged bits
the pen, so mighty strong
condemned, oh yes, you have no chance
to prove who's right or wrong

The mighty Pen has caused such pain
If used in such a way
to tear a soul in shredded bits
to make a soul pay

Destruction of a soul by words
It seems a mighty shame
but all by words, the mighty pen
destroy another's name

So loosely used, these words unkind
some men so cruel be
the mighty Pen has said it all
for all the world to see

So careful friend, when pen is used
Lest some poor soul should die
a little more within because
the pen, the reason why

So kill and maim, destroy within
It's easy with the Pen
it has the power, a might itself
the message it can send

Oh words and pen, destructive force
In hands of wicked men
The sword no match, nor never be
Against the Mighty Pen.

Roy V. Benson

NOW I LAY ME

As now I lay me down to sleep
This prayer be yet today
for nothing more could say it all
This simple prayer to say

As now I lay me down to sleep
These words stayed through the years
These words mean more each passing year
These words grow ever dear

As now I lay me down to sleep
Revive and think each word
for really friend, it's quite a prayer
The simplest ever heard

As now I lay me down to sleep
I rest my soul in Thee
If morning light should not be mine
My Soul up there shall be

As now I lay me down to sleep
The Lord my Soul to rest
and should I die before I wake
My Father He Knows Best

A FOE BECOMES A FRIEND

This message I would like to leave
Speak kind of other men
for many times you will behold
a foe becomes a friend

And tear not down your fellowman
Don't speak unless be kind
We'll plant more seeds along the way
then better harvests find

Let us look for good in man
in each in his own way
So let us guard so carefully
the words we say today

For words we sow that we shall reap
Each word return to us
so let me say and think good things
The harvest, may I trust

Roy V. Benson

I PITY

I pity the person for things that you have
I pity the person that stands in your path
I pity the person he'll suffer your wrath
I pity the person

I pity the person he'll suffer the day
I pity the person those words that you say
I pity the person you'll make him pay
I pity the person

I pity the person it's all in your game
I pity the person destroy a good name
I pity the person you'll never know the shame
I pity the person

I pity the person this game that you play
I pity the person that stands in your way
I pity the person I'm sorry to say
I pity the person

WEATHERED TOWNS

'Tis sad to see these weathered towns
The people getting old
Buildings of the yesteryears
Such stories could be told

The young must leave for better things
The future here is bleak
They move to higher plains they trust
Their futures there to seek

Old weathered town of days gone by
What blessed history
If only folks could just have seen
How grand you used to be

"THERE was papa John's big home
His daughter was so fair
And Mary Lou lived down the street
Around the corner there."

Roy V. Benson

MEMORIES

Memories of yesteryear
How rapidly they fade
We soon forget just how and why
These memories were made

How pleasant memories become
Each passing of the years
It seems so very long ago
These memories so dear

Each little thought can mean so much
Reach out into the past
Memories they soon become
If only they could last

Of yesteryears, how long ago
We wish they always be
But now they fade with passing time
They're getting hard to see

So memories be kind to me
My dreams let linger on
and yet I know they soon will end
They too will soon be gone

10 FEET TALL

A boy, someday a man to be
this lad with a pleasant smile
No cares, for life is full indeed
And life is well worthwhile

He's happy for each morn that comes
Another day ahead
With hopes and plans it's new to him
And many miles he'll tread

Each friend he'll greet with "Hiya Pal"
They'll scheme with something new
And set about with mighty plans
These days that's all too few.

Of course, there's days of studies too
Some chores along the way
But he will learn it must be so
But yet his mind will stray

What pleasant days, these boyhood days
When life is but a dream
Of well laid plans, so big indeed
And many prankish schemes

But then it quickly passes by
A man, we find at last
And out of these our memories draw
They're yesterdays that's past

And now he goes, a man within
We're proud he's done so well
And as we look at other boys
This story seems to tell

Roy V. Benson

So this is life, it never ends
Thank God for boys so small
I'll bet they think they're mighty big
They're all of 10 feet tall

THESE DAYS

The day will come and could be soon
For man, his sins he'll pay
It seems as though the world gets worse
Each passing of each day

The Porno kings, the use of drugs
Destruction on mankind
It really seems we do not want
A better life to find

People sue, and kill with joy
The wars, no end to show
And others want their pleasures first
And always on the go

The young can't cope and suicides
They seem to claim their share
I wonder really what goes on
I wonder if we care

Abandoned boys and girls alike
By millions, turned away
We live and close our eyes to those
In blindness life each day

Oh yes, I know that some will say
The problems are not mine
But they are wrong for me we must share
Each problem that we find

So if there is a slightest chance
Reach out and show you care
For all must reach a hand to help
For all must do their share

CHILDHOOD DAYS

Remember well those childhood days
When life seemed all-aglow
With play and frolic everyday
And always on the go.

We have much in earthly things
A home we called our own
Some food to eat and little else
And clothes with patches sewn

We thought of games to pass the time
Or hike the yonder hills
With slingshots in our pockets crammed
We never could stand still

"Complain", why never heard the word
each day we lived with joy
it wasn't much like things today
there hardly was a toy.

Yet we grew up, a happy lot
We went from morn till night
Just gone where mom could never tread
We never were in sight.

But when the hunger pains increased
We somehow found our way
Back to that place that we called home
At the ending of the day.

We had our dreams like all boys have
Someday a man we'd be
And we'd go here or yonder there
This world was ours to see.

Well, childhood days are long since gone
Not all those dreams came true
For quickly pass the days to years
The years that's all too few

Roy V. Benson

FRIENDS

I look on back into the years
Nigh 60 years or so
And wonder what I treasure most
Those things that I can show

I cannot count my riches great
For riches passed me by
Nor can I count the things I've done
As castles in the sky

But I can count much greater still
Than gold could ever show
Just friends, they're great, I count
A privilege to know

The things of earth could never buy
The friendship of a friend
For he will always see you through
Be with you till the end.

OH WHAT WORDS

What words we say to other folks
In anger or in haste
And never once give any thought
Just how these words must taste.

Destroy their names with words we use
No thought is given there
We only think of precious self
We live and do not care

It matter not if gossip, friend
Or suits we name them in
We only know our side is right
And we will surely win

Destroy their names, we never think
Or do we really care
We're only thinking of ourselves
We only want our share

So gossip not, it will return
Each hurt we'll surely bear
For every word returns to us
What then becomes our share?

TUESDAY MORNING SIX A.M.

It's Tuesday morning six A.M.
The coffee's boiling there
I wonder what the day will hold
Be cloudy or be fair

I do not know each step I'll take
The people that I'll greet
I only pray that strength I have
Each challenge that I meet

Tuesday morning six A.M.
What paths my life will take
Be wise in all I think and do
Decisions that I make

I pray I live it wisely Lord
I pray each word I say
Will grow a harvest great to see
To live for other days

So Tuesday morn at six A.M.
My prayer be here on earth
Each one I meet and words I say
Be weighed for what they're worth

Another cup of coffee friend
Another brand new day
Another walk through paths unknown
I pray to find my way.

I PRAY

I pray I treat my fellowman
As I would want to be
That acts and deeds in all I do
Be Lord, as unto Thee

I pray my words be true within
In kindness that I speak
That I will never wound a heart
Revenge, I'll never seek

I pray that all I do or say
Be done with spirit kind
Thy goodness I will find

HELP US FATHER

Help us father, now I pray
Help us father, every day
Help us when we're weak within
Give us victory to win

Help erase these inner fears
Let us feel Thy presence near
Give us strength for every task
Hear our prayers, we humbly ask

Give to us the will to try
Not that we may inward die
Learn to count each blessing dear
Freedom from all want and fear

Let our love be true till death
And every day by Thee be blessed
That our lives may grateful be
And life's beauty learn to see

HELP US LORD

Help us Lord to walk upright
To not lose sight
To better things
In everything

Help us Lord through every trial
Through every mile
When things go wrong
That we be strong

Help us Lord when we should call
If we should fall
To rise anew
This life be true

Help us Lord when lonely here
Erase our fears
When nights are long
To find a song

Help us Lord though weak we be
Find strength in Thee
In every trial
Through every mile

Help us Lord our love to give
Our love to live
That we be kind
Our purpose find

Help us Lord each day to grow
Each seed we sow
In love they be
Their goodness see

Roy V. Benson

Help us Lord though weak within
Each battle win
Through every day
Along life's way

Help us Lord through daily chores
To seek Thee more
When day is done
This race we run

Help us Lord with vision clear
To hold that dear
Each value know
Thy love to show

Help us Lord our troubled minds
Thy peace to find
When others cry
Not pass them by

Help us Lord when life is O'er
To Heavenly shores
To know Thy will
Thy purpose fill

MY PRAYER

I pray My Lord, to grant to me
Not homes, nor things of wealth
Nor things the world has value on
Nor things to glory self

I pray my Lord, to better be
To live, forgive and trust
In things of Thee, not things of earth
That I be true and just.

O grant me Lord, compassion now
O give to me Thy love
Impart in me Thy spirit now
Thy spirit from above

Understanding, Lord I want
Patience, grant to me
A humble heart of thankfulness
To wait, my Lord, on Thee

Roy V. Benson

CURSING

I met a man the other day
He cursed, the Blessed name
His grammar was quite horrible
It really was a shame

I felt quite sorry for this man
The word he used in vain
For every other word, I think
He cursed the Holy Name

To think that he shall some day stand
And answer for each time
He cursed the Lord, His Blessed Name
Excuses then to find

So careful friend don't curse that name
His name be Christ the King
But carry high, his banner high
And praises to Him sing

Escape you'll never know my friend
A sorry man you'll be
A record there for every time
Each time you cursed, to see

WORTHY?

I live for the time of Christ's return
The rapture in the sky
And what a day, my friend, will be
To be ushered in on high

Oh, I'm not worthy of this gift
My sins have not been few
But Christ atoned my sins for me
To give me life anew

It's very hard to comprehend
A King do this for me
The only way, my only hope
This Heaven ever see

A King, A King, forgives my sins
Worthy? No my friend
And yet he loved enough to die
With Him, our lives to spend

So as I humbly give my thanks
And as I realize
This gift I'm far from worthy of
My sins, A King would die

And now He lives and intercedes
I'm far from perfect yet
But oh to think this King, my Christ
My sins in love forgets

Roy V. Benson

TIME OF DAY

Armageddon near at hand
Perhaps, I do not know
It seems as though the day is late
Later than it shows

Man is acting rather strange
No leaders anywhere
With people living as they wish
And no one really cares

Countries are in strife and pain
Hunger still abounds
The olive branch is waved aloft
But yet no peace be found

Oh peace they cry and how they wish
But peace eludes them all
This pride of man still marches on
It goes before the fall

Some will think to hide their heads
These thoughts too negative
They'd rather not give any thought
The days ahead they live

But they are like the man that builds
His home be built on sand
And when the trials may come his way
His home will never stand

So time of day, what be the hour
It's not for me to know
But all the things that's going on
The time of day it shows

JUDGE ME NOT

Don't judge me yet, my friend I ask
You see my Lord has quite a task
He's molding me most every day
So judge me not, my friend I pray

A lot of work must yet be done
You see my Lord has just begun
And it won't be till that heaven gain
For up till then, you judge in vain

A perfect soul I'll never claim
My human nature's still the same
But God is changing everyday
This life I live, into His ways

So judge me not is my advice
For each old habit slowly dies
But you can judge when God is done
For only then, these battles won

But in the meantime, you see
A far from perfect man in me
So judge me not my friend I ask
For God's still working on the task

Roy V. Benson

THE BRIEFCASE

Into this world, I arrived alone
A stranger, a babe as well
Here I would walk, seeds I would plant
A journey, my life to tell

I had no things or earthly gains
The briefcase was empty here
I did not as in certain tones
Now give to me my share

This empty case, not even clothed
This earth, a stranger her
A helpless soul in a mighty land
Too weak to really care

I learned it fast, these few short years
My briefcase, I would stuff
And gather things unto myself
When would there be enough

But then it comes, to say good-bye
This briefcase, cannot take
We leave this earth just as we come
All gone, this life we made.

So foolish one, your briefcase fill
Fight on, count not the cost
another man your case will find
Your gains for you are lost

That briefcase filled, a few short years
And then the Judgment Day
You'll leave this world as you arrived
There is no other way.

An empty case when you arrived
The same, when life is o'er
So think my friend, what is the worth
Those things you're fighting for

Yes, We shall stand, every man
Before the Great White Throne
We shall be as we arrived
For we shall stand alone

A briefcase filled of earthly things
I wonder what their cost
If we shall hear "depart my friend"
Without Christ, our life is lost.

Roy V. Benson

LIFESTYLES

I read of styles, such living styles
Where endless wealth abounds
Where all these things just seem to flow
No earthly wants be found

They give a pittance just to brag
To show the world they care
But what they give this pittance small
Is such a little share

God doth expect, the more we have
The more we are to give
To help another hurting soul
Somehow, his life to live.

So you of means, such earthly means
What will your answer be
"There were no hurting souls, Lord
These souls I did not see."

These things you count so very dear
One day, will be our naught
And you will see the folly of
The life on earth you bought

So have these things, enjoy them well
These things so big and great
For on that Day, The Judgment Day
It all will be too late.

GOD'S BOOKS

The day will come, my friend, for all
God's books be open wide
Each deed, each act, or friends we've tread
There's nothing we can hide.

We'll all have many reasons why
We did a selfish act
Or why we took which wasn't ours
On others turned our back

Each lie, each cheat, each evil thought
Is all recorded there
The way we treat our fellow man
The days we didn't care

God's books record our life on earth
Escape, we'll never know
Our sinful evil ways be there
On earth, the life we sowed

Be careful friend, God's books record
How we did run the race
For each man's acts will all be there
God's books we'll surely face

IT IS WRITTEN

For it is written, we shall die
And then the Judgment Day
When all mankind though big or small
His life to then be weighed

The masses will weigh in far short
The few, the scales bend
It's up to you and you alone
Eternity to spend.

Those written words, that man shall die
To some bring hope and cheer
And others tremble at the thought
Eternity to fear.

And yet there are those that give no thought
Tomorrow never comes
But yet that little word says "all"
It never said "for some"

The written word will not depart
It haunts unto the end
Be careful, for it's up to you
Eternity to spend?

SO GRANTED

So granted, how we take this life
So granted, take each day
So granted, we must surely think
So granted, is our way

So granted, for the food we eat
So granted, for our health
So granted, for the things of life
So granted, for our wealth

So granted, for the trees in bloom
So granted, for the rain
So granted, for the birds in the air
So granted, be our name

So granted, for the sun that shines
So granted, for the storms
So granted, for the lakes and streams
So granted, is the storm

So granted, all these things of earth
So granted, we shall live
So granted, take for everything
So granted, never give

So granted, will one day be ceased
So granted, be the end
So granted, we should now give thanks
So granted, time to spend

So granted, we are foolish men
So granted, is our way
So granted, this would never end
YET GRANTED IS THIS DAY.

NO THANKS

What small and puny men we are
No thanks for life to give
But take each blessing as though it's ours
A selfish life to live

No thanks for food before us spread
No thanks for health itself
Too busy Lord, I guess we are
To gather things of wealth

Too busy just to pause in thanks
Ungrateful creatures we
I'm sure when He looks down on us
Ungratefulness He sees

Too busy with the things about
No prayer of thanks above
But take for granted all these things
The blessings of His love

I pray that I, for one will learn
To give My thanks to Thee
In all things Lord, the big and small
My life may grateful be.

PUGET SOUND

I've traveled here, I've traveled there
But no where yet I've found
Where God did bless, the earth as much
Than right on Puget's Sound

We have the sun to warm its shores
The rains to keep it green
With mountains capped majestically
Such beauty to be seen.

There's every type of outdoor sport
A mile or two away
It truly is a paradise
In which to work or play

So let me spend the years ahead
Near shores of Puget Sound
For if I searched the world o'er
No nicer could be found

WE CREATURES SMALL

What little creature we must be
No thanks to ever give
But think these blessing always were
As selfishly we live

We find so many things that's wrong
The weather or the day
Or maybe just the neighbors cat
Our words in anger say

Well maybe someone slighted us
We'll do the same to him
We'll go about and maybe talk
Than try his friendship win.

It seems so easy just to gripe
As down life's road we go
We'd never think to look above
In thanks for life to show

It surely must displease our Lord
That gave it all in love
When we ungrateful creatures won't
Just pause to look above.

EARTH'S BEAUTY

Don't reach into the starry skies
Until you've mastered earth
You'll find so many things right here
Such beauty of much worth

It is not earth that be at fault
Unpleasant things you see
It's true that man has made a mess
With this we all agree

But yet there's beauty all around
Creation's grand display
You never see the two same things
It's just creation's way

It seem that man must sometimes look
Beyond, into the blue
To wander way from troubled things
Refresh our soul anew

You see my friend, the earth is good
There's beauty everywhere
God made this planet and He gave
To us, His love to share

So look about, appreciate
It's all so very free
For all the beauty of this earth
It's here, for you and me

THE BLAME

Excuses there be hard to find
If only we could blame
Another man for things we've done
Or only use his name

If I could point my finger then
Persuade the Judge that day
"It wasn't me, it was that man
He led me, Lord, astray."

But no my friend, it's yours to have
To answer for your sins
So careful friend the game you play
This game if you should win

A LOSER

You stretched the truth, perhaps a bit
The lie, it wasn't meant
You really thought it for the best
The truth, be slightly bent

You thought it'd never come to light
You never meant no harm
Perhaps it all would go away
And never cause alarm.

A scheme or two, you think you'll do
As greed becomes your game
But you will list far more my friend
And there's no one to blame.

No, my friend, it will not die
Each lie must come to light
And you would wiser be my friend
If you had done what's right.

But this is not the way of man
For self, he's placed it first
It grows within and can't be quenched
This selfish inner thirst.

So if you've gained by little lies
The rules you knew to bend
You are my friend, a loser now
A loser in the end.

ROADS

This life that we live
A choice we must make
Of paths we must tread
And roads that we take

Some other folks blame
Their background in life
But who's lived it all
Without any strife

It's true there's a few
Protected each day
But friend would you want
To live life this way

This life we go through
Will be what we choose
Some folks will gain
While others will lose

So paths that we tread
And roads that we take
Some folks must they bend
While other may break

The choice lies ahead
Decisions to make
I pray that your road
Be the right road to take

WORDS CALLED BACK

If every word we could call back
And issue them anew
I wonder if we'd say so much
Or if our words be few

We say such words we can never mean
But yet in haste we say
We'd never have to sorry be
If every word we weighed

So words called back, it would be nice
Impossible my friend
So let us know so very well
Each word, a message sends

What message do we wish to send
What message on our mind
We are within the words we say
The words that others find

So every word will leave a mark
Be kind the words you say
For all the words that you have said
Return to you someday

Each man is guilty of this sin
Of idle words in vain
Of hollow praise to others say
To others causing pain.

But all these words cannot be called
Each word my friend, will stay
So therefore ever careful be
The things we do and say.

Roy V. Benson

WE'VE GATHERED FOLKS

The folks have gathered round the church
The passing of a friend
How very little thought we gave
Today would be the end.

If we could change that yesterday
Now that today is here
I wonder what we'd do and say
This friend, we counted dear

We gather round with silent hearts
Too late, what we would say
It always seems we'll get around
These things, another day

That other day is here my friend
Our voices silent now
We meant so well that yesterday
But never knew quite how

A lesson learned, I doubt it so
So quickly out of mind
Until the day we stand again
A day like to this to find.

WHAT A LIFE

Attorneys tear with words unkind
Destroy just all they can
They glory in their job, my friend
Destroying fellowman

It seems so strange to live that way
To wake up every morn
To think ahead and plot the day
What lives today be torn

No thought is given to the words
No thought of damage there
They only live to win their case
For others, do not care

Accusations that are made
Though they may be untrue
Creates a wound that never heals
To leave a scar anew

These scholars of the law they're called
What wonton hurt they give
It seems so very odd to me
The life they chose to live.

BROTHER'S KEEPER

Am I my brother's keeper, Lord
To help, if he should fall
To lend a hand, example be
To heed his beckoning call?

Why can't I live for self alone
Forget the other man
To live as I would dare to live
Not give a helping hand?

Must I think that others look
And wonder what they see
I wonder if, what they may see
Is pleasing Lord, to Thee

Examples, patterns for a life
Will someone look at me
And say "I'd like to be like him"
"My life like him to be"

If I should be a pattern Lord
I pray this pattern show
A life that will not lead astray
Some other one I know

THINK IT THROUGH

Don't place your dreams, your hope, your charms
On things that pass away
For what you have is quickly gone
It's yours for but a day.

Yes, beauty comes, all gone too soon
What memories we share
Did we walk for self alone
For others, did we care?

What is our goal, our purpose here
What seeds of love were sown
What did we do for fellowman
What joys of life were shown

O ye that live for self alone
May God have pity them
When turned away from Heaven's door
Eternity to spend?

It all will be for all to see
That life we spent on earth
Just what our treasures meant to us
Just what we counted worth.

O friend, it comes so very soon
Our ways we must amend
For it is up to us alone
Eternity to spend?

Roy V. Benson

THE ROADMAP OF A LIFE

A babe is born, to journey forth
The highways of this life
To face each day that lies ahead
Its joys, its fears, its strife.

What roadmap will you give this child
What paths will he tread there
What words of wealth, what will you say
What joys or grief to bear?

It's up to you there's no one else
To shed a guiding light
It's up to you, your words and deeds
Ne'er he should lose his sight

A map, for roads lead many ways
Some strewn with grief and pain
Temptation's snares, where evil lurks
Where life is lived in vain

A map of life, each road ahead
May it be full and free
So as you, friend, look back upon
A life of joy you'll see

I WONDER

I wonder what these people think
That rob and steal and take
And think no thoughts of words they've said
The troubles that they make

They live today, no thoughts beyond
I guess they'll never learn
But oh they cry and carry on
When then the table turns

It all goes back to just one thing
It haunts us to our grave
That what we sow is what we reap
From this, no man be saved

So let us sow with kindly words
With acts and all our deeds
To think not of ourselves alone
But think of others' needs.

Don't take what is not yours to count
Don't think of only "me"
For you will never gain a thing
No happiness you'll see.

Roy V. Benson

TO KNOW

To know which way this life to walk
To find the good therein
Where does the strength, the better life
Where does this life begin

To find the trust in fellow man
To look upon that one
To know that love is but a seed
To die if left alone

Do better things, a better way
Just grow without a cause
Or must we gather strength within
So as not suffer loss?

And if we lose what have we gained
A loss, what good can be?
If we but choose the loss ourselves
What harvest do we see?

A love that's ours, O let us guard
With life, if this we must
Let's never do a foolish thing
To break this faith and trust.

ONLY THE GOOD LORD KNOWS

Only the good Lord sees ahead
The very paths upon I tread
The words in kindness that are said
Only the Good Lord knows

Only the Good Lord knows each day
That I may walk in righteous ways
That He may guide me, this I pray
Only the Good Lord knows

Only the Good Lord know my mind
Each word, and action, each its kind
They may be good, I pray He finds
Only the Good Lord knows

Only the Good Lord gives His best
I pray His strength for every test
That through me other lives be blessed
Only the Good Lord knows.

Roy V. Benson

WHY COMPLAIN

I'm not complaining about my life
It's really served me quite well
It's had its hurts, an arrow or two
And some things I'd rather not tell

I've had my hurts, many a hurt
It seems as they're not over yet
But rather than dwell on unpleasant things
These things I'd rather forget

I'm sure we've all had a problem or two
These things we must forget and forgive
And look at each day with freshness anew
Each day we're privileged to live

I don't really think our problems are anew
I'm certain they've been lived before
So look on the good, the bright day ahead
Who knows what life has in store.

SINKING SHIPS

Some lives be as sinking ships
So hard to stay afloat
They drift around and never find
The rescue of their boat

They're looking for the rescuer
But look, it seems in vain
They really want that helping hand
And rescue be their gain

Sinking ships on seas of life
They slip beneath the waves
And only God will ever know
The numbers lost each day

Perhaps you know a sinking ship
A lifeline throw them there
For sinking ships it's up to us
To show them that we care

Roy V. Benson

RUSSIAN ROULETTE

Oh what a pity, oh what a shame
Just watching you play that dangerous game
No thought of your soul, Eternity where?
I think you would mind, I think you would care

Russian Roulette, has nothing on you
Each day that goes by, grows fewer and few
No thought do you give, it's as you didn't care
I'd think you would think of Eternity where

A dangerous game, a pity, a shame
The life that you live, to live it in vain
Escape you may think, I'm sorry my friend
Escape knows you not, you'll see in the end

So Russian Roulette, the game be in vain
Forgiveness is yours, then Heaven to gain
But go it alone and surely you'll lose
Remember each day, a fewer for you

Oh what a pity, oh what a shame
You'd better forget, this dangerous game
Your life to proclaim, to Jesus in love
And then you will reign, in Heaven above.

IF I TOLD YOU

If I told you of a place
With streets of solid gold
Where man lives on eternally
And never there grow old

If I told you of a place
No tears, no hurt, be there
I'm sure you'd want to be a part
This place, you'd want to share

If I told you of a place
With gates of solid pearl
It sounds unreal, it sounds too much
A dream beyond this world

If I told you of a place
No tears, no death, no pain
What would you give to be a part
Your entry there to gain?

If I told you of a place
A mansion on this street
And it be yours forevermore
This mansion yours to keep

If I told you of a place
Where joy and love abounds
My friend, you'll never hurt again
No heartaches there be found

If I told you of a place
Where all these things be true
And they wait there for you to claim
They're watching there for you

171

Roy V. Benson

If I told you of a place
There's one thing you must do
Accept My Lord in humble faith
This love He gives to you

So I have told you of this place
Joint heirs with Christ to be
This place He offers you my friend
In love so full and free

So if you now know of this place
What are you waiting for
It's yours to claim, to be a part
To claim forevermore

Now that you know, why hesitate
Why wait another day
Accept His love, repent my friend
There is no other way

So I have told you of this place
Decision time is yours
Remember friend of what you choose
You choose forevermore

So when I walk the streets of gold
I pray I see you there
Decision time, so choose it right
Then all these joys we'll share

Jerusalem, the name to be called
The City of My Lord
I know it's there, I know it's true
I read it in His Word

So if you laugh and lose my friend
Believe no one His word
Then blame yourself, you did not want
Believe in what you heard

I know it sounds just like a dream
But what if I am right
And you reject and laugh it off
Your entry not in sight

So please I beg, don't close the door
This place, it's waiting there
Just answer yes, accept this Christ
This place be yours to share

I ask you friend, consider this
Could you afford the cost
For you alone, the loser be
Your soul forever lost.

Roy V. Benson

SLIPPING ABOUT

I've slipped and stumbled many times
And lost my way as well
But Christ was there to lift me up
More times than I can tell

I'd like to live to sin no more
A perfect man to be
But if this so, No Christ I'd need
From sin to set me free

No, it's much better that He died
From sin to set us free
For then we'll be with Christ above
With Him, eternally

So don't you fret, if you should slip
You'll never be perfect
You'll always slip and stumble some
Until your Lord you see

You see my friend, if you sinned not
The Cross would be in vain
You'd surely be a loser then
With nothing as your gain

So thankful be that He is there
To lift you when you fall
To hear you cry in loving care
To hear when you call

EDUCATED FOOLS

Educated fools roam
Upon this earth below
They roam so others plainly see
Their education shows

No common sense for many men
The books did not teach well
For if you watch them closely friend
A fool, his actions tell

I've seen these educated men
So foolish in their ways
And yet their education rules
In things they do and say

So education, it is great
But common sense must play
A real vital part in life
To live success each day

Roy V. Benson

THE BRAGGART

Braggart small or braggart large
How great we think we are
With puffed up minds and swollen pride
The world's greatest star.

We love to brag and others tell
Of all the mighty things
Our exploits there and exploits have
Our praises love to sing

But all is gone, it matters not
The piper we must pay
We cannot say to go away
Please come some other day

Then all our bragging selfish self
To dust, our bodies go
And soon forgotten, oh so soon
No legacy to show

So puff yourself oh foolish man
Do brag your foolish ways
For all is gone, how great you were
There on your dying day.

The world moves on, it stands still not
The end comes all too soon
There'll be another one to sing
To sing your every tune.

VENGEANCE AND HATE

Vengeance and hate
The things that you do
Remember, my friend
Returns unto you.

Vengeance and hate
The words come my way
Vengeance and hate
The words that we say

Vengeance is ours
We recklessly aim
Another to hurt
It's part of the game

Of how it may hurt
The vengeance you give
Blind to the fact
The vengeance you live

Vengeance is hate
What a pity my friend
Vengeance and hate
Is the message you send

Eaten by vengeance
Oh what a shame
You're hurting yourself
By playing this game

Oh what a pity
Man and his way
Eaten by vengeance
Another to pay

Roy V. Benson

Destroy as we will
Another man's soul
Not counting the cost
Not counting the toll

Eaten by vengeance
Consumed deep within
Never a thought
The hurt it may bring

Vengeance will rob
Any good that you see
It closes your eyes
To be blind as can be

So what do you want
Vengeance and hate?
Open your eyes
Before it's too late

If vengeance is yours
I pity you friend
For vengeance consumes
Right to the end

Yet man is consumed
By vengeance and hate
Oh what a shame in vengeance we wait

Each man has a choice
The life that he lives
You'll only return
The portion you give

A man can expect
To reap what he sows
So satisfied be
By the harvest that shows

"Vengeance is mine"
Thus saith the Lord
Believe it or not
It's told in His word

So throw out your hate
For vengeance is sin
And thereby your life
A new life begin

Roy V. Benson

YOUR ACTIONS

The actions you show
It maybe outside
But the actions you show
Is a mirror inside

The actions you show
Or hide if you may
Be careful my friend
You'll give it away

Your actions mean much
In all that you do
Your actions you know
A reflection of you

So all of those words
And things that you do
Are only my friend
This mirror of you

WOW

Imagine this, it's Judgment Day
Before the Judge we stand
And then too late a finger point
And blame another man.

Each deed we've done or left undone
Will haunt us on that day
Some will lose and some will win
There is no other way

Those words what damage we will see
If only we had known
And now we stand before the judge
We stand so all alone

Imagine friend, before too late
What will your answer be
For every man there comes a time
To face eternity

So Judgment Day, we've gathered there
Our lives before our eyes
For it's appointed every man
Yes, everyone to die

So all we've done, each word we've said
Each hurt to fellowman
Recorded there for all to see
In Judgment we shall stand

Roy V. Benson

ESCAPE

Escape my friend, you never will
Escape that Judgment Day
There's millions like escape as well
They'd love to know a way

It's certain friend, that Judgment Day
Appointed, man to die
We'll all be there, yes everyone
That Judgment Day on High

If only man could find a way
Escape that Judgment Day
So know for certain Judgment be
From life, the very start

Alternative, you have my friend
Acceptance of the Lord
Believe and trust, your only hope
Foretold within His Word

Decision time, what will it be
Your chances you will take?
Escape you'll never know my friend
And then it be too late.

CREATION'S PLAN

The eagle soars into the clouds
Up to such starry heights
What graceful beauty on the wing
As he soars out of sight

What beauty God's creation tells
The birds on wings of air
And only God in love so kind
Create such beauty rare

So give Him praise in everything
Creation's story told
The eagle's flight in yonder sky
Creation there unfolds

Creation's story, beauties rare
As only God can plan
To think He masterminded it
And gave it unto man

"Dominion over," God did say
"My plan I give to you
Be kind and guard creation's plan
Be kind in all you do."

Roy V. Benson

CAN'T DO MUCH OF ANYTHING

I cannot make the flowers in spring
I cannot make the sparrows sing
I cannot make the birds on wing
I cannot do much of anything

I cannot make the oceans roar
I cannot make the ocean shores
I cannot make the clouds that soar
I can't do much of anything

I cannot make stars on high
I cannot make the starry skies
I cannot make the clouds drift by
I can't do much of anything

I cannot make the time too slow
I cannot make the time to go
I cannot make each season show
I can't do much of anything

I cannot make the snow so white
I cannot make the day so bright
I cannot make the dark of night
I can't do much of anything

I cannot stop the wind blow
I cannot stop just where they go
I cannot stop their whispering
I can't do much of anything

I cannot understand just why
Or how the clouds hang in the sky
Or stop the eagle soaring high
I can't do much of anything

I cannot fly like birds of prey
I cannot understand their ways
Or how they float up there on wings
I can't do much of anything

I cannot understand just why
Some will live and some will die
Paupers some and others king
I cannot understand these things

Amazed I stand in all these things
I know so little of anything
But I look up to God on high
He surely knows the reason why

Roy V. Benson

CREATION'S WAY

Into each life some rain must fall
That statement is quite true
We're never promised sun to shine
With Heaven always blue

The clouds will come and they too pass
Some storms along the way
But if we realize, my Friend
The sun's not far away

A trial or two is like a storm
It's ominous and grey
But it will pass and we shall see
The sun to come our way

So if the rain could gather there
The sun is not in view
Have heart my friends, the sun will shine
Tomorrow's day is new

HARKEN THE NEW DAY

I've walked in gardens soft with dew
I've smelled the morning air
I've listened to the bird's sweet song
And beauties so wondrous fair

I've seen the morning sun just peek
O'er yonder hills away
To tell this story to mankind
It's now another day

I've heard the morning come to life
When flowers sing their song
In beauty seen them raise their heads
They've slept the whole night long

What peaceful beauty there to find
In gardens soft with dew
When nature harkens praise above
This day so fresh and new.

Roy V. Benson

SUCH BEAUTY RARE

I live above a windy bluff
The sea is far below
I see the greatest show on earth
Creation's story told

The gulls, their graceful flight in air
The waves against the shore
One day a wind, the next a breeze
For us, created for.

Creation's story, oh what love
To see this beauty rare
That God should love to let me see
His beauty I should share

What beauty there before my eyes
It's all a joy to live
I hope that I in turn can find
A thanks for life to give.

Index

Printed in the United States
73137LV00003B/145-153